13 British Artists
Children Should Know

Alison Baverstock

PRESTEL

Munich · London · New York

Contents

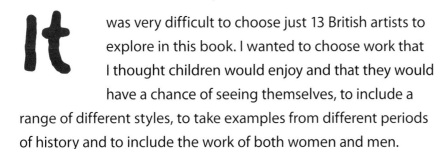 was very difficult to choose just 13 British artists to explore in this book. I wanted to choose work that I thought children would enjoy and that they would have a chance of seeing themselves, to include a range of different styles, to take examples from different periods of history and to include the work of both women and men.

Though this book is about these 13 artists rather than the history of art, some ideas keep cropping up, such as the influences that shaped the artists' early lives, the training they received (or didn't) and whether or not their families encouraged them. One interesting theme is that the artists featured in this book were often not seen as particularly talented in their own time. Perhaps this was because the artists were doing something unexpected or different, but perhaps it was because those who saw their work felt uncomfortable, or did not know how to describe it.

To learn more I suggest you try to look at art in person by visiting museums, art galleries and art in public spaces. Think about visiting a part of the collection or a specific exhibition that is not familiar to you. Learning to appreciate something new can make you feel really creative, and might help you to come up with good ideas of your own.

If you feel that a particular artist has been unkindly overlooked, write to me at Prestel telling me why, and we may consider an appendix of 'near misses' for a future edition of this book. You could also look at Prestel's bigger book *50 British Artists You Should Know*, which will hopefully make you realise how difficult my task of selecting just 13 really was.

Technical terms* are explained here

The Artist's Husband, Charles Beale in a Black Hat, c. 1670
Private collection

Having a portrait painted was often an important stage in building a family's reputation. Today we are used to family photographs and more informal recording. Where do you keep records of how your family looked? In great houses open to the public, the most usual place for displaying the family portraits is in the entrance hall. Why do you think this is?

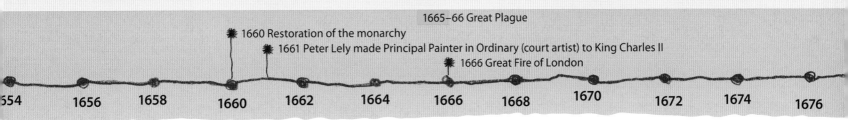

Mary Beale

The wealthy and important commissioned her to paint their portraits. Now what she saw is how we remember them

Born:
  1633, Barrow, Suffolk
Lived in:
  London
Died:
  1699, London
Known for:
  Portraits*
Children:
  Bartholomew and Charles

Mary Beale lived in exciting times. She was nine when the English Civil War broke out, which lead to the execution of King Charles I. She moved from London to the countryside to escape the Great Plague of 1665–66 and hence also avoided the Great Fire of London, which followed shortly afterwards.

Although she is often described as one of the most important portrait painters of 17th-century England, it is just as significant that she was also the first female English professional painter. At a time when few women had careers, being an artist – let alone a successful one – was most unusual. She was taught to paint by her father, himself an amateur artist, who also paid a tutor to teach her.

In 1652 she married Charles Beale, a cloth merchant and amateur painter. He was not successful in business and in 1665 they moved from London to Hampshire to save money. But in 1670 they came back to London and set up a portrait studio together, with Charles managing the business and mixing the paints, Mary doing the painting and their two sons first helping out and later painting too.

Aphra Behn, c. 1670
St Hilda's College, Oxford University

A portrait is a picture of an individual but also a historical document. Most people choose to be painted in their best clothes, so if we know when a portrait was painted, we can also see what jewellery and clothes were fashionable then.

Born:
28 November 1757,
London
Died:
12 August 1827,
London
Lived in:
London and Felpham,
Sussex
Known for:
Painting, printmaking
and poetry
Children:
None

William Blake

Even when first created, Blake's work was seen as 'different'. But today it still feels so fresh that many people do not realise he lived over 200 years ago

William Blake's images are much better known than his name, and you may also know his poetry – the words of the hymn 'Jerusalem' or his most famous poem, 'The Tyger', which begins 'Tyger, Tyger, burning bright'. Because his work is so very different from that of other artists, still feels modern and remains well known through posters, greetings cards and book illustrations, it is difficult to decide how he fits into the story of art. His contemporaries had the same problem.

From childhood onwards William had visions: first of angels and later of his brother Robert, whom he nursed until Robert died from tuberculosis. He had a very strong sense of good and evil and was particularly interested in how the world was created. All these ideas appear in his art.

Blake's work was so different and strong that it frightened people, and many responded by criticising it, or dismissing him as mad. He lived at a very turbulent time in history, during the French Revolution, the American War of Independence and the anti-slavery movement. In his writing he challenged society: for example, he highlighted the injustice of sending poor children to clean the chimneys of richer people. Artists today have also used their work to protest about issues such as war, child labour and lack of care for the environment.

Newton, c. 1795
Tate Britain, London

Blake has been criticised for showing bodies that are not anatomically correct: they have extra muscles in places. Do you think this matters, or is an artist free to depart from nature for effect?

1833 Slavery Abolition Act passed by UK Parliament

1817 Dulwich Picture Gallery, the first purpose-built art gallery, opens in the UK
1818 Mary Shelley publishes *Frankenstein* (anonymously)

300 1805 1810 1815 1820 1825 1830 1835 1840 1845 1850 1855

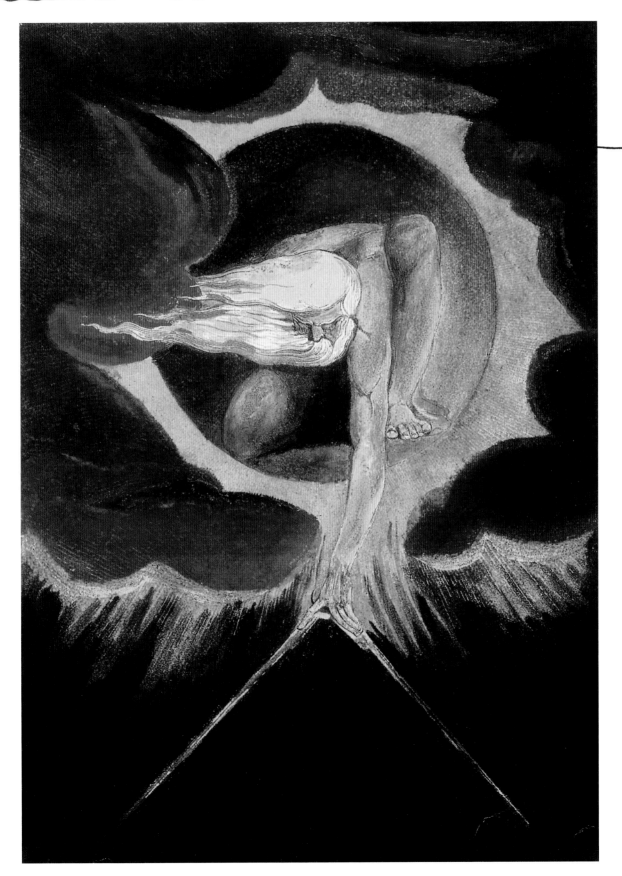

The Ancient of Days, 1794
Glasgow University Library

Look out for the sense of strength in Blake's work. We see powerful people making sweeping movements and emphatic gestures. You will also see warm colours in his pictures, which are vivid and bright.

Tip
Blake earned his living by making and selling prints. Some were book illustrations, and others were pictures for general sale. Prints were cheap to reproduce, so many copies could be made and sold. Beryl Cook's work (see pages 26–27) was made famous in the same way, largely through greetings cards, which sold to those who do not buy art or visit galleries.

Snowstorm – Steam Boat off a Harbour's Mouth making Signals in Shallow Water, and Going by the Lead, 1842
Tate Britain, London

Turner is often called the Father of Impressionism*. The picture *Snowstorm* gives us a really good impression of how a storm at sea might look and feel, as opposed to showing what we know is there. This is similar to the work of the French Impressionist artists.

J.M.W. Turner

A prolific artist – today often
hailed as the 'Father of Impressionism'

Born:
  23 April 1775, London
Died:
  19 December 1851,
  Chelsea
Full name:
  Joseph Mallord
  William Turner
Known for:
  Landscapes
  and seascapes
Children:
  Evelina
  and Georgiana

Being an artist was originally a job that you learnt as an apprentice, but in the 18th century it became more common for artists to learn their craft in academies, or art schools. J.M.W. Turner's father was an impoverished London barber, but at the age of 14 Turner became the youngest student ever to enter the Royal Academy Schools* in London. He exhibited his first watercolour a year later, in 1790, and began to work on oil paintings too.

In 1796 Turner exhibited an oil painting, which was a turning point in his career. The picture, *Fishermen at Sea*, shows a boat struggling against an increasingly difficult sea, by the light of the moon. Many of his future paintings echoed these ingredients: an emphasis on light, hazy back-grounds and dramatic movement. As time went on, his paintings became increasingly sketchy, which was probably the result of his failing eyesight.

Having had little money as a child Turner worried about his finances, spent very little on personal comfort and lived in what his contemporaries described as 'squalor'. Many of his fellow artists admired his work but did not like him. But he was very proud of his growing reputation, considering himself the best artist of his time – 'I am the great lion of the day.'

Artists are not always easy people to live with. Whatever their art form (writing, painting, acting, playing), it is often the case that those whose genius is admired find it difficult to get on with other people. Do you think this matters? Should knowing what other people thought of an artist influence how we appreciate his or her work?

**Rain, Steam and Speed –
The Great Western
Railway, 1844**
National Gallery, London

Children often start
pictures by drawing a
blue sky at the top of the
page and green grass at
the bottom. Turner used a
huge number of colours,
especially in his skies
and seas. How many can
you see? Some of them
may surprise you, since
we don't think of the sky
as displaying so many
colours. Look out for the
movement in his pictures
too. Previous landscape
painters had captured
the stillness of the
environment, but Turner
is a showman who gives
us action.

Tip
Look up the work of the
French Impressionists (for
example, Monet, Sisley or
Pissarro) and compare it
with that of Turner. Look
in particular at the range
of colours they all use.
Which artists are most
reliant on sunshine?

Born:
  8 June 1829,
  Southhampton
Died:
  13 August 1896,
  London
Lived in:
  London and Perth,
  Scotland
Known for:
  Pictures that tell a
  story, portraits and
  landscapes
Children:
  Everett, George, Effie,
  Mary, Alice, Geoffroy,
  John, Sophia

Tip
Millais' parents
encouraged his art. They
moved to London to let
him attend art school
and gave him a perfectly
fitted-out studio in which
to work. You might like
to compare his path
to becoming an artist
with that of Leonora
Carrington (pages 24–25).

John Everett Millais

It is often said that 'every picture tells a story', but some
are easier to read than others. Millais' work is easy to relate
to – and enduringly popular

Millais was a child prodigy who went to the Royal Academy Schools* at
the age of 11. But once there he found being so much younger than
the other students difficult; he was bullied for his precocious talent and
privileged background.

In 1848, when he was 19, he became a founder member of the
Pre-Raphaelite Brotherhood, a group of painters who set themselves
up against the Royal Academy and tried to return to a simpler art. They
wanted to make their work feel more intensely real, to study and paint
outside the studio and to capture the vivid colours and details of nature.
The group members produced many of today's most popular paintings
in art galleries, often basing them on a familiar story or moral. Eventually
each member developed their own style and they painted together less.

In the 1870s Millais began to concentrate on painting portraits* and
landscapes. He was a successful book and magazine illustrator, and also
created stained-glass windows. He worked hard to support his eight
children. But what had been radical in his early life grew more accepted,
and just before his death he was elected President of the Royal Academy,
the organisation he had so opposed when he was a young man.

1896 Millais elected President of the Royal Academy

65   1870   1875   1880   1885   1890   1895   1900   1905   1910   1915   1920

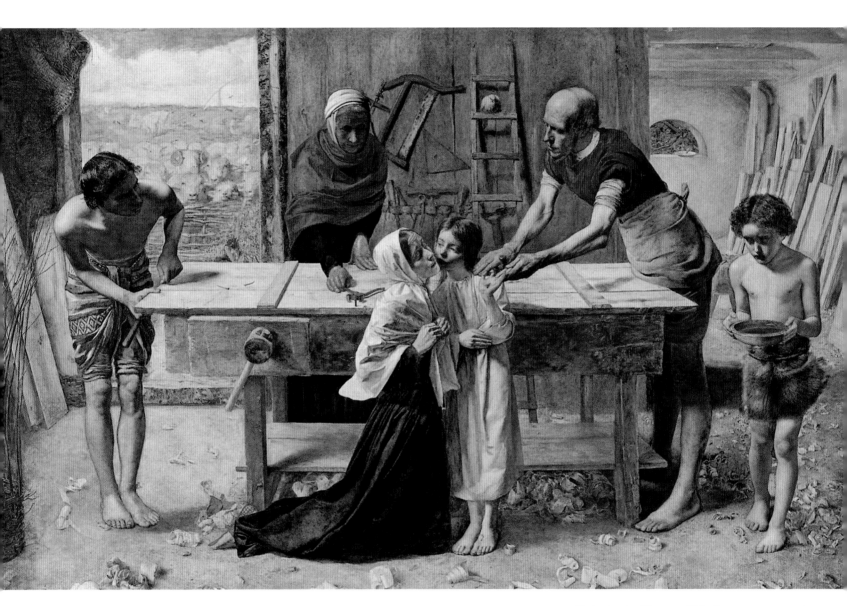

Christ in the House of His Parents, 1849–50
Tate Britain, London

This painting was derided in the press as ugly. Do you think that this in fact helped Millais, by making his work famous? Can you think of an example of someone who has become famous through being criticised?

Ophelia, 1851–52
Tate Britain, London

Look out for the detailed backgrounds in Millais' pictures, which show a strong awareness of nature. In *Ophelia* the plants look like a horticultural study. The artist is giving us far more detail than we would be able to see if we were to stand in front of the river. To try this, stand outside and concentrate really hard on what is in front of you. What is at the edge of your vision? Can you see the detail without turning your head to look properly? In Millais' outdoor pictures, every aspect of the picture is shown in high detail.

The Cripples, 1949
The Lowry Collection, Salford

Much of Lowry's work shows figures and buildings in a space that does not have much depth (this is called 'two-dimensional'). Yet perhaps that is a closer reflection of how we really see the world around us. For example, the people and organisations that affect us most loom much larger in our consciousness – maybe your school looks larger to you than it really is. Perhaps his vision is closer to our experience of the world.

L. S. Lowry

The creator of 'matchstick men and matchstick cats and dogs' – who never achieved the recognition in his lifetime that he has today

Born:
1 November 1887, Salford, near Manchester
Died:
23 February 1976, Glossop, Derbyshire
Lived:
Manchester and Hyde, Cheshire
Children:
None

above:
Head of a Man, 1938
The Lowry Collection, Salford

L. S. Lowry's paintings are so very different from work by other artists of his time, and his style is so instantly recognisable, that people often assume he was self-taught. In fact, although he was turned down for art school, and worked throughout his life in a series of financial jobs, he took art lessons for many years and was eventually recognised by the art world that for a long time had thought his work childish and odd.

Laurence Stephen Lowry was a loner. An only child, he never married, and later looked after his widowed and disabled mother until her death, but he would paint after work in the evenings, and at weekends. What he recorded were the daily goings-on of the world in which he lived, the industrial north of England, which had not been made the subject of art before.

He died aged 88 in 1976, just months before an exhibition looking back at his life's work opened at the Royal Academy* in London (this is called a retrospective exhibition*). It broke all attendance records for a 20th-century artist. Salford Museum & Art Gallery began collecting his work in 1936 and today house the collection in a building named after him.

We have become used to art being about certain things: beautiful views, illustrations of stories from history or plays, flowers and portraits. Yet when someone presents us with a view of a scene we take for granted, we start to notice the details in a new way. What do you see every day that you have never seen as the subject of a picture in an art gallery? Perhaps the inside of a supermarket or a hairdressing salon?

Coming from the Mill, 1930
The Lowry Collection, Salford

At first, art critics often commented on the 'simplicity' of Lowry's pictures, and yet if you look at them in close detail there is a lot going on. Sketches show that he took great care in laying out his work. In reproductions of his paintings on birthday cards or posters the colours look flat and single-shaded, a bit like in 'painting by numbers'*. But if you have the chance to see one in real life you will find that his pictures do not have the smooth surfaces we see in reproductions; the paint is laid on thickly and individual brush strokes can be seen.

Tip
If you like the work of this artist you should look up the art of Pieter Breugel the Elder, who also painted street scenes and village life – but 400 years earlier. If you want to see the kind of pictures Lowry liked, see the information on Millais (pages 12–15). Lowry saw paintings by the Pre-Raphaelite Brotherhood in Manchester and his favourite artist was Dante Gabriel Rossetti, some of whose work he eventually bought.

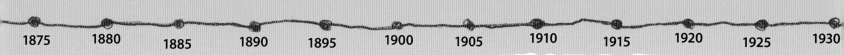

Born:
30 July 1898,
Castleford,
West Yorkshire

Died:
31 August 1986,
Perry Green,
Much Hadham,
Hertfordshire

Lived:
Castleford, Leeds,
London, Perry Green

Children:
One daughter, Mary

Good to know

The surfaces of Moore's sculptures have an interesting feel to them; some parts are marked with tiny scratches and others are smooth. Although his sculptures are huge, they make us want to touch them.

Henry Moore

Moore's long career offers us a series of work that stretches, toffee-like, between pressure points. The lines become simpler, the spaces larger, but their impact never lessens

Henry Moore came from a mining family, but his father was determined his own children should not be miners. After school Henry taught, but in 1917 he went to London to enlist in the Army. He visited the British Museum and was excited by his first view of art from around the world.

Injured in a gas attack, Moore recovered but spent the rest of the war as a physical training instructor. Once home he enrolled in Leeds School of Art to study sculpture, although no student at Leeds had done this before. From there he won a scholarship to the Royal College of Art* in London.

His work was unlike anything produced by a British sculptor before: huge rounded shapes that mostly show the human body. There are certain themes he returned to many times, such as *Mother and Child* and the human body lying down (or reclining). His later work became more abstract* (which means it did not relate specifically to things we can identify).

Having experienced what war is really like, the likelihood of another depressed him. He became an official war artist* during the Second World War and drew Londoners trying to carry on with their lives.

Moore liked to work in stone, wood and bronze, as well as to draw and engrave. Today his work is on display worldwide, and continues to influence us.

King and Queen, 1952/53
W. J. Keswick Collection, Glenkiln

The heads of Moore's sculptures are often lacking in the details we might expect, so it is up to us to provide the stories that go with them. For example, in *King and Queen* the two figures are looking in slightly different directions. Are they seeing the same thing? Do they look regal or isolated? Are they talking to each other?

Three Piece Reclining Figure: Draped, 1975
(LH 655)
Collection of the Henry Moore Foundation

Moore's stone sculptures suggest the human body rather than providing all the anatomical detail, and he emphasises certain parts of the body more than others. For example, this reclining figure emphasises the joints on which the body would be supported – the elbow, buttocks and knees – and the strength of the shoulders is highlighted by the space beneath them. In later sculptures the figure is sometimes conveyed through quite separate pieces of stone or bronze; yet even when divided, we can still see a single reclining body.

Should public art be voted for? If everyone has to see something, should we all have a say in what is displayed? How could this best be managed? Compare this with the work of Antony Gormley (pages 32–35).

Leonora Carrington 1917–2011

1914–18 First World War

1939–45 Second World War

1924 Surrealist Manifesto published

1939 Sigmund Freud dies

1895   1900   1905   1910   1915   1920   1925   1930   1935   1940   1945   195

Leonora Carrington

A Surrealist artist who lays out a treasure trove for us to examine in further detail – and in the process stokes our imagination

Born:
6 April 1917, Clayton Green, near Chorley, Lancashire
Died:
25 May 2011, Mexico City
Lived:
London, Paris, New York, Mexico City
Children:
Two sons, Gabriel and Pablo
Style:
Surrealism

Leonora came from a wealthy family in Lancashire but spent most her life living far from there. She ran away to Paris with the Surrealist* artist Max Ernst, then went to Spain and to Mexico City where, apart from some time in New York, she lived from then on.

Her parents were not artistic and she was unhappy at home. She thought that creativity comes from within the individual, not from the genes they inherit. But she did remember the stories told her by her Irish nanny.

Her work is surreal, full of mysterious figures and situations, parts of which we half-recognise, but in combinations that seem just out of reach. They remind us of pictures that illustrate books of myths and legends which we have heard before but can't quite remember.

Carrington refused to explain more, to give up the mystery and tell us what was in her mind when she painted each picture. 'The visual world is not an intellectual game', she said. Without her to tell us what is happening, we have to make up our own meanings. So everyone who looks at these pictures will think about and remember them in a different way.

Many of Carrington's pictures look like stage sets on which the figures have been placed with great care. Ask someone of your parents' age if they remember being given rub-down transfer books as children, where there was an empty background and you had to decide which characters went where.

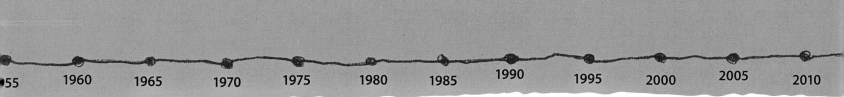

The Giantess, also known as The Guardian of the Egg, c. 1947
Private collection

Look out for the gentle, daydreamy feel of her paintings. What do you think is happening? The characters shimmer; they float in a calm background that seems to hold them, like when you 'pause' a film on screen. What happens when the gallery is closed – do you think they move?

Tip
Leonora Carrington's pictures are packed with details. But nothing is ordinary: the horses may have wings, and the birds very exotic plumage or human faces.

Compare them with the detail in Millais' *Ophelia* (pages 14–15), which is a very precise recording of nature. The work of both artists is full of details, but they are very different in style and approach.

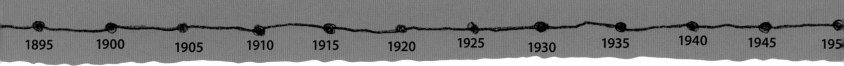

Balletomanes, c. 1980, Private collection

Notice how the hands are large and bloated – a bit like the foam ones that get handed out at sporting fixtures to hold up at key moments – but they are also carefully drawn. The woman choosing a chocolate at the ballet is making two pincer movements at the same time to extract the chocolates she wants.

Beryl Cook

'I suspect Beryl Cook's painting will be remembered and cherished long after most 20th-century artists are forgotten.' Edward Lucie-Smith, art critic*

Beryl Cook's paintings are much loved and instantly recognisable, but she did not go to art school, and did not start painting until she was in her thirties. She first learned to paint using her son's paint-box and whatever was available to paint on (cardboard, paper, fire-screens and even a breadboard!). She had a precise ability to spot how people stand, and in particular how they relate to each other in groups. She also loved to get the details of their clothes, shoes and expressions right.

Beryl had three sisters, and went to an all-girls' school. She left school at 14 and worked in theatre and the fashion trade. She and her husband lived in Africa, later returned to the UK and settled in Plymouth with its noise, vibrant bars, returning sailors and tattoo parlours.

All these influences can be seen in her pictures. Her work is full of people, and she liked to show us parties and in particular groups of women enjoying themselves. She points out the absurdities of life, but her work is never unkind; she smiles at people rather than making fun of them. She makes us smile back. Her work is completely original: no one else paints quite like her.

Born:
10 September 1926, Epsom, Surrey
Died:
28 May 2008, Plymouth
Lived:
Reading, London, Zimbabwe, Cornwall, Plymouth
Children:
One son, John

Tip
Fashion models may be very thin, but the reality is that most people are fatter. Compare the figures in Cook's pictures with the stick-like figures of L. S. Lowry (pages 16–19) and in galleries with the work of Peter Paul Rubens and Stanley Spencer.

Beryl Cook used the life around her. She spotted situations that amused her and objects that appealed to her, and put them together in pictures that make us smile. But she did not start painting until the middle of her life. Do you know anyone who has long wanted to produce art, but has not yet done so?

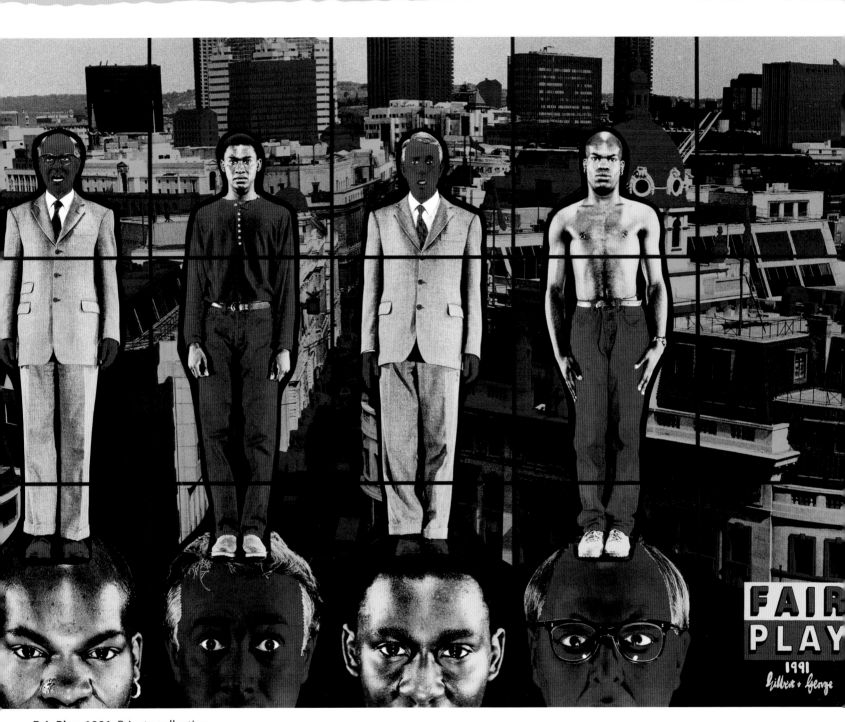

Fair Play, 1991, Private collection

The subjects dealt with by Gilbert & George are sometimes very unusual and often shock people. Can you make art out of anything? Is there any subject or incident that should not be the basis of a work of art?

Gilbert & George are often described as being different, and another way of saying that is to say that their work is highly individual and original. But they are two people. Is it possible to be an individual when you are creating something that is shared? Can the art of two people really be described as being by one artist?

Gilbert & George

In their own words: 'We are two people but one artist.'

Live:
 The East End
 of London
Studied:
 Both studied
 sculpture at
 St Martin's School
 of Art, London
Known for:
 Large-scale pictures,
 being 'Living Sculp-
 tures', wearing suits

Italian-born Gilbert and English-born George met at art school in London on 25 September 1967 and have created art together ever since. They have turned their lives into an ongoing art experience and have become 'Living Sculptures'. They live together – and are rarely seen apart – wear near matching suits, speak slowly without interrupting each other, and coordinate the way they move to produce a synchronised art form.

Their art centres on whatever currently interests and affects them. Each subject is explored in detail. They examine what they select with intensity, sometimes with a microscope, and try to find patterns and meaning in it. Their pictures are large, using negative images to create their sometimes huge trademark pictures. These are coloured very brightly and overlaid with a grid-like graph. The overall effect can look like a very modern, secular stained-glass window.

The art of Gilbert & George is always created by them together, in collaboration*. When they exhibited the first *Charcoal on Paper Sculpture* they created together in 1971, reviewers tried to work out which artist had created which bit of the picture, but now their art is seen as having shared authorship.

Tip
The Pre-Raphaelite Brotherhood were protesting about art getting too distant from nature. Blake (see pages 6–7) used his work to protest about conditions he found unacceptable, especially for children. George said: 'We never protest against anything, we protest for things.'

No one individual can ever truly know how it feels to be someone else. If you were going to live and work as closely with someone else as Gilbert & George do, what aspects of your life would you have to coordinate? Would you eat the same things and go to bed at the same time? What would happen if one of you were hungry or tired and the other were not?

Garrowby Hill, 1998, Museum of Fine Arts, Boston

Hockney gives us a sense of what it might be like to freewheel down this road on a bicycle, with the road running away in front of you. The road curves a bit like a Scalextric set. Let your eye travel along it from the bottom left-hand corner, towards the bend by the trees. Can you feel your shoulders start to sway?

From the hill, your eye is drawn along the road and away into the distance. The lines on the fields make the 'pull' feel even stronger. Like Dorothy in *The Wizard of Oz*, you just can't help following the road – although hers was made of yellow bricks, not grey-blue ones.

David Hockney

An internationally famous artist, working in lots of different media. But whatever format he chooses, the response of artists, art critics and the general public alike tends to be very positive

Born:
   9 July 1937, Bradford
Lived:
   London, Los Angeles, Bridlington in Yorkshire
Known for:
   Working in many different media, including digital art produced on an iPad

Born in Yorkshire, David Hockney knew from an early age that he wanted to be an artist. He studied first at the Bradford School of Art and later at the Royal College of Art* in London. Here members of staff are allowed to purchase the work of just a few students each year, and Hockney's talent was spotted. His work still hangs in the main room used to entertain visitors.

Hockney is famous for being a really good draughtsman, which means that his work is very well put together (art critics* might say it is 'well executed'). For example, in his pictures the people seem to stand in real space, and the landscapes offer depth* and a feeling of substance. He paints trees very well, which is much harder than it looks.

He works in lots of different artistic styles and media, including portraits*, landscapes, painting, collage, printmaking, graphic art, stage design and photography. Whatever his medium, his work tends to attract the admiration of both people who know a lot about art (whether artists or art critics), and members of the general public who find his work easy to relate to, and very memorable.

Quiz
If you look carefully, the landscape opposite can be divided into different sections, according to groups of similar colours used. Why do you think this is?

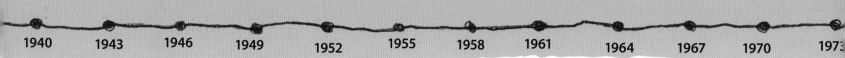

Born:
30 August 1950, London

Studied:
Trinity College, Cambridge; also studied Buddhism in India and Sri Lanka

Known for:
Sculpture

Children:
Three children

Tip

What does it mean for work to be 'made from the inside, from the other side of appearance'?

Perhaps Gormley means thinking about how someone can present themselves to the world in order to give a real sense of what it is like to be them (something we can never truly know about someone else).

Antony Gormley

Offers us figures in the landscape who occupy the space so completely that we stand and stare – rather than wonder why they are there

Antony Gormley is a sculptor whose work is usually based on the human body, often his own. He considers the space around his sculptures to be just as important as the sculptures themselves, and enjoys siting his work in unexpected places.

Gormley has talked about his work being 'made from the inside, from the other side of appearance, celebrating a moment of being in time'. His method of creating work illustrates this. In order to capture the shape of his body for a sculpture, the artist has to begin by being still himself. Gormley wraps materials around himself that will capture his shape and then uses these to make a 'cast' or mould that can provide the outline of the sculpture.

Sculptures that are made to stand in the open air, and that can withstand both weather and other hazards (such as animals and birds, incoming tides or low-flying aircraft), need to be still, strong and silent, and require little looking after. This is very different from our day-to-day world where things move quickly and everything is replaceable. If you look at Gormley's work, it just is. It is calm, quiet and serene.

From the beginning of his career, the public and the press have been fascinated by Gormley's work. He draws our attention, but neither he nor his sculptures tell us how to look at them, or what we are supposed to see. We cannot ignore them, but they do not tell us what to think. And while the landscape and sky change, we too are still.

Angel of the North, 1995/98
Gateshead

Traditionally angels bring happy news or give protection. This figure feels benign, but its enormous wing span is quite inflexible and it would be difficult to find shelter here (unless it could slope or roll up its wings). The site, near Gateshead, is a former coal mine, where generations of local people had worked underground. Is the Sculpture calling us to remember those who needed protection in the past, or offering us a symbol of calm in a hectic hub of road and rail?

When it was first commissioned in 1995, and put up in 1998, there was a lot of controversy, but now many local people are proud of it, and their children look out for 'our angel' to tell them how close they are to home.

Another Place, 1997
Installation view, Cuxhaven, Germany

Another Place is a series of 100 cast iron figures now installed on Crosby Beach, near Liverpool. The figures, again based on the artist, face out to sea over a 3.2 km stretch of sand. As the tide comes in the figures disappear, one by one. All the figures are impassive and quiet, and their re-appearance as the tide gradually goes out again is mysterious.

Field for the British Isles, 1993
Installation view, Irish Museum of Modern Art, Dublin

In 1994 Gormley was awarded the Turner Prize* for a range of his work including *Field for the British Isles*, a series of tiny figures that look up at the viewer, and which can be installed in various places. Several schools have copied this idea, giving every pupil the same amount of clay and asking each to create a little figure which is displayed with all the others. By putting all the figures in a space at the same time, and without a human to provide a sense of scale, the figures look much larger than they are in real life.

1940 1943 1946 1949 1952 1955 1958 1961 1964 1967 1970 197

The Distance (A Kiss with String Attached), 2003
Tate Britain, London

The Kiss is a very famous sculpture by the French artist Rodin which had been in the Tate Gallery for a long time. Cornelia Parker wrapped it in string. The arms of the two people kissing each other used to form the boundaries of the piece, but now the string adds another layer. The string is loose, so could be wriggled out of, but it still restrains the two figures. But then we remember that they cannot move in any case – because this is a sculpture, not real life.

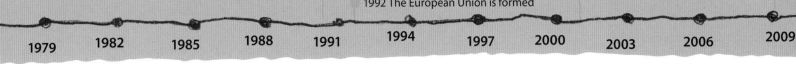
Cornelia Parker

An artist who works with everyday items – but subjects them to change. And in the process she makes us see them in a new light

Born:
  1956 in Cheshire
Lives:
  London
Known for:
  Installations
Children:
  One daughter, Lily

Cornelia Parker was born and grew up in rural Cheshire, to the south of Manchester. Her parents had a 'smallholding', a piece of land on which they grew crops and raised animals, and her help was needed. She has many early memories of the bitter cold and the cotton twine with which she had to tie up hundreds of tomato plants. It was hard work, and to take her mind off it she would daydream.

Her work is often described as 'installation art' or 'site-specific art'*, which means that it is created for a particular place and does not stay there forever. Her work also celebrates familiar objects: things that we take for granted and so do not tend to look at in detail, but which can gain a new meaning when they are lifted out of their everyday setting, subjected to change and carefully lit.

The installation that made her famous is called *Cold Dark Matter: An Exploded View* (1991). It was displayed in the Tate Modern in 2000. To make this she took an ordinary garden shed, filled it with the kind of things people store in sheds, and moved it to the middle of a field, where she asked the Army to blow it up for her. She photographed the explosion frame by frame, so she could see what happened. She collected up all the pieces and hung them by fine wire from the ceiling of a gallery around

Shared Fate, 1998
Artist's collection

In *Shared Fate* Parker was given
access to the guillotine that
was used in 1793 to execute
the French Queen, Marie
Antoinette. She used it to chop
a range of other things in half –
a newspaper, a doll and a loaf
of bread. There is a guillotine on
display in the National Museum
of Scotland in Edinburgh but
people keep their distance.
Knowing that this artist has
touched the blade that killed so
many people, and then used it
to cut things in half herself,
sends a shiver down my spine.

**Cold Dark Matter:
An Exploded View, 1991**

a light bulb, with small fragmented objects in the centre, then the middle-sized ones, and finally the larger pieces and the wood of the shed. Some parts of the original can still be identified (such as the window, and panels from the roof). The light hung in the middle shows where the explosion took place, creating dramatic shadows on the floor, walls and ceiling of the exhibition space. The result is a shimmering collection of material that is still roughly shed-shaped, but with a new dynamism.

Parker's ideas are bigger than just the work created. All the pieces described for you so far are interesting in themselves, without you needing to see what they look like. The public have responded by wanting to catch sight of her installations before they slip away and are lost to us forever.

Tip
It was on a school trip to London that Cornelia saw the art galleries and museums for the first time, and this made her want to be an artist. Henry Moore (see pages 20–23) also found seeing the museums in London for the first time a life-changing experience.

Nelson's Ship in a Bottle, 2010, Trafalgar Square, London

In 2009 Shonibare MBE provided a sculpture for the fourth plinth in Trafalgar Square: a recreation of Nelson's flagship, HMS *Victory*, but this time in a bottle. The recreation was completely as might have been expected, apart from the sails, for which he used more 'African'-looking fabric, making the international links clear. He left people to wonder how the ship got into the bottle!

2002 The Euro becomes the currency of many European countries ✾

2010 David Cameron
becomes Prime Minister of the UK ✾

2001 The World Trade Center in New York is bombed ✾

1994 Nelson Mandela is elected President of South Africa ✾

82   1984   1986   1988   1990   1993   1996   1999   2002   2005   2008   2011

Yinka Shonibare MBE

Shonibare MBE plays with images we know already – and then makes changes. Now in bright fabrics and three dimensions, no longer can we assume all was as it seemed

Yinka Shonibare MBE was born in the UK but moved to Nigeria when he was three, and spent most of his childhood there. He returned to London to go to art school. He has now made his home in the East End of London, and his work includes sculpture, paintings, poetry and performance art. He considers himself bi-cultural, influenced by all aspects of the various cultures in which he has lived and aware of the political, economic and social overlappings of class, race and life around him.

Although he thinks that artists are often unaware of what goes into their work, he is interested in how different traditions become merged. For example, the brightly coloured batik fabrics that are used in much of his work are traditionally associated with Africa. But, although popular there, they were in fact developed in Indonesia, exported to England and the Netherlands, and then sold to African merchants. In the same way, artistic influences converge and overlap, and no one can be entirely sure where ideas come from.

Quiz
Why do you think the artist calls himself Yinka Shonibare MBE?

Born:
1962 in London
Lived:
Lagos, Nigeria, and London
Known for:
Sculpture, installations, painting and photography
Children:
One son, Kayode

Black Gold II, 2006

Black Gold II presents a series of round circles of material on a thick black background that looks a bit like a large patch of oil. The mixture of things that don't normally go together - fabric from clothing and oil - seems political; perhaps it is a reference to the value (in both people and recources) that can be extracted from countries that are colonised.

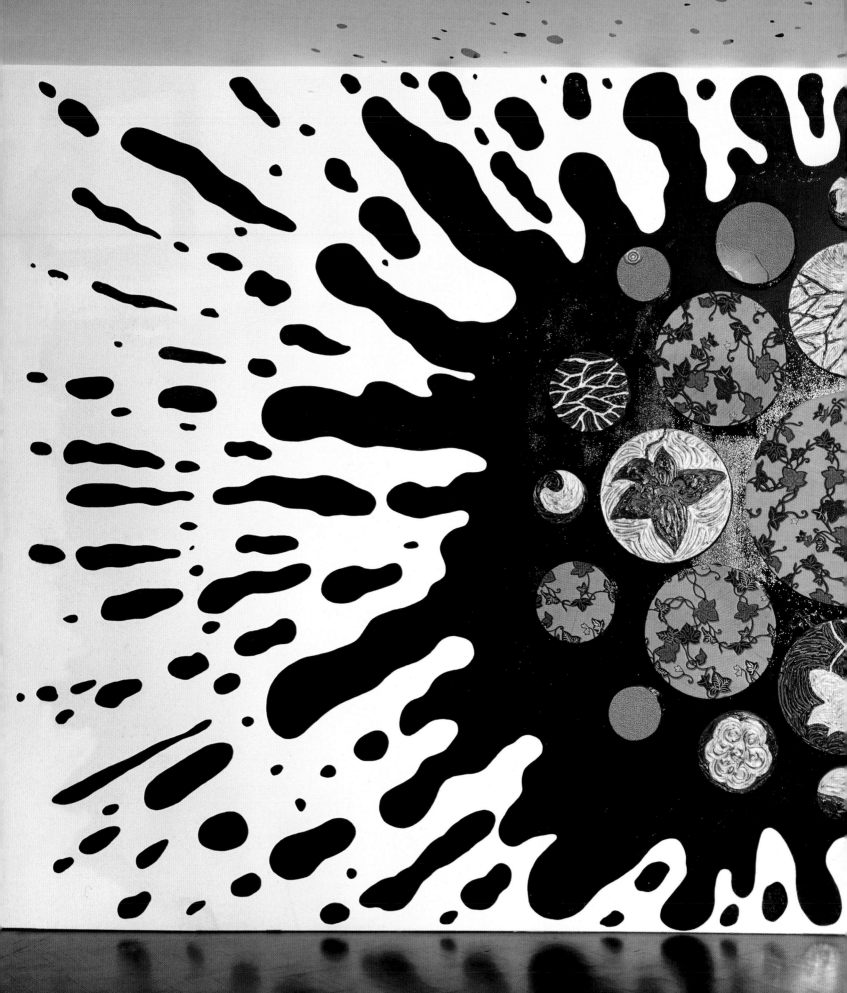

Glossary

ABSTRACT ART does not relate specifically to things we can identify. It is often contrasted with figurative art, which is representational (that means it is based on real things). But this simple description does not mean to say that abstract art cannot remind us of things or suggest shapes to us, or that figurative work is always easy to read.

ACCESSIBLE means available to as many people as possible. 'Accessible art' is a term often used to indicate work that ordinary people, and in particular those without prior experience or expertise, find easy to understand or appreciate. For example, pictures which offer us a clear story, or have a title that tells us what to look for, are often referred to as accessible. This is because the viewer can make sense of what is presented, and think about what the artist was trying to achieve (although this may differ from what was in the artist's mind – if indeed he or she is willing to tell us!)

ART CRITICS are journalists who write or talk about art, mostly through newspapers, radio and television. They often have particular preferences that they share with their audience. While they can have a big effect on an artist's career and popularity at the time of writing, in the longer term we do not always think they are right.

COLLABORATION involves working with others to achieve a particular goal. Collaborative art is usually the result of sharing ideas and developing them together.

This is not as easy as it sounds. Any creative project can be developed in lots of possible directions; compromising to suit everyone can reduce the 'wholeness' of what is produced, while maintaining commitment to a path you were not keen on can be tricky. The key is often to have enough discussion so that everyone feel involved. If you manage to create a team which works towards a common goal, and no one can remember exactly who did which bit, you have true creative collaboration.

DEPTH in art often refers to the representation of space, or three dimensions, on a flat surface that has only two dimensions. Artists have used various techniques to convey depth in their work: for example, they might use different palettes of colour for different sections of a landscape, make objects in the distance smaller, or use more detailed brushwork on objects close to the viewer.

IMPRESSIONISM began as a term of abuse in the late 19th century, when an art critic in France took the word from the title of a painting by Monet and used it to sneer at the work of a group of artists who liked to paint out of doors, and to capture a quick 'impression' of the light and movement they observed. The subject-matter they chose was often ordinary – they painted each other having picnics, sitting on the beach or in bars. Today the work of Impressionist artists such as Monet, Renoir and Pissarro are often the most popular with the public.

INSTALLATION or **SITE-SPECIFIC ART** is work that is created for a particular place, and will not stay there forever. Once dismantled, although it can be kept and may be displayed again, it can never be reassembled in exactly the same way.

RETROSPECTIVE A 'retrospective' is short for 'retrospective exhibition', which is one that looks back at an artist's whole career. This is usually organised late in their working lives, or perhaps just after they have died.

OLD MASTERS A commonly used term for skilled artists working in Europe before about 1800. Before there were art schools, many artists learned their craft through being apprenticed to master artists.

ONE-PERSON (or ONE-MAN) SHOW A show that concentrates on just one artist – as opposed to shows that feature the work of several. Being offered a one-person show is a mark of success.

PAINTING BY NUMBERS kits were popular when the author of this book was growing up! A kit consisted of a board marked out into separate areas, each of which contained a number, together with a range of paint pots and a list showing you which numbers referred to which colours. If you filled in the numbered areas with the right paints you ended up with a complete picture. Kits were often based on famous paintings – so in the process you created your own copy.

PORTRAIT A representation of an individual in art: perhaps a painting, a photograph or a sculpture. A good portrait may tell us what someone looked like at a particular point in their life (we call this a good 'likeness'), but can also reveal much more – their personality or mood, and what they consider significant (the clothes and jewellery they wear, and which background or accompanying objects they chose to be shown with). The choice of artist to produce a portrait is very significant. For example, try to find out how many portraits have been produced of Queen Elizabeth II, and how different they look – although they all show the same person.

PUBLIC ART is art in public spaces, accessible to all, rather than being in art galleries or the homes of individual owners. You can see examples of it in this book from Henry Moore, Antony Gormley, Cornelia Parker and Yinka Shonibare MBE.

THE ROYAL ACADEMY OF ARTS was founded in London in 1768 to promote art through education and exhibition. It was intended to help raise standards and encourage the public to appreciate good work, and had an associated school and a library to train artists. However, it became associated with the development of 'official standards'. Since artists often try to produce something new, many came to see the Academy as a point of departure for their own work (see the pages on Turner and Millais). Each summer the Royal Academy still hosts a big art exhibition of current work, which is much enjoyed.

THE ROYAL COLLEGE OF ART in London is the world's only completely postgraduate university of art and design – you can only attend if you already have a degree (or the equivalent) from somewhere else. Although it is called a college of art, its students work in many areas, including car and industrial design, architecture and fashion.

STILL-LIFE refers to art that shows inanimate objects, or those that do not move. Still-lifes commonly feature fruit, flowers and sometimes china, glass or musical instruments. It is a very old art form – there are still-life images on the walls of ancient Egyptian tombs.

SURREALISM was a movement that began in the 1920s. Surrealists worked in various art forms; there were Surrealist writers as well as Surrealist artists. There have been attempts to list the elements of Surrealist work, and these have included surprise and the putting together of unconnected things in strange combinations. The prefix 'sur-' on a word means additional or extra (hence 'surcharge') and surreal art is often art that feels extra-real – or dreamlike. Surreal art is often better spotted than explained, and in this book you will find the work of the Surrealist artist Leonora Carrington. The figures float in a space that is not quite real, and though they relate to reality, they are clearly products of the artist's imagination.

TURNER PRIZE When J.M.W. Turner died he left a large number of paintings and drawings to the nation, and this is housed as The Turner Bequest in Tate Britain. A competition is run annually in his name to celebrate innovation in art. Several of those nominated, and one winner, are featured in this book.

WAR ARTISTS Traditionally words described the experience of war, in books and newspapers, but war artists offer an additional way for those not involved to visualise an experience most people will never have first-hand. Some war artists are officially commissioned by government or political groups, and others are people who are there anyway – and keep a record of what they have seen. The earliest war artists provided images of the Crimean War (1853–56). The sculptor Henry Moore became an official war artist during the Second World War; his drawings of people sleeping in lines on the platforms of the London Underground are unforgettable.

For Neil, Alasdair, Jack and Hamish. Thank you for (mostly) listening.

Answers to the quiz questions

page 31: Traditionally landscape painters, often called 'the old masters'*, painted the ground in three colour segments to create a sense of distance. The sequence was generally green for the foreground, brown for the middle distance and blue for what was far away. Look out for landscapes by artists such as Claude Lorrain and Nicolas Poussin in art galleries and you can spot this. Although the road runs through Hockney's picture like a river, and is always the same colour, in the rest of the picture he has used a colour scheme to create depth*: red and green for the foreground, yellow for the middle distance and blue for far away.

page 41: Shonibare was awarded the MBE (Most Excellent Order of the British Empire) in 2004 and was so proud that he uses the letters as part of his name (most people who receive such an honour feature the letters after their name). The official name for these letters is post-nominals.

Library of Congress Control Number is available; British Library Cataloguing-in-Publication Data: a catalogue record for this book is available from the British Library; Deutsche Nationalbibliothek holds a record of this publication in the Deutsche Nationalbibliografie; detailed bibliographical data can be found under: http://dnb.ddb.de

Photo credits:
The illustrations in this publication have been kindly provided by the museums, institutions and archives mentioned in the captions, or taken from the Publisher's archive, with the exception of the following: p. 20, 21, 22/23: reproduced by permission of The Henry Moore Foundation, Photograph p. 22/23: James Copper; p. 24: akg-images/Marion Kalter; p. 30: © David Hockney, photograph: Museum of Fine Arts, Boston; p. 31: © David Hockney, Photograph: Jean-Pierre Goncalves de Lima; p. 32: Oak Taylor-Smith; p. 33: Colin Cuthbert, Newcastle; p. 34: Helmut Kunde, Kiel.

Prestel, a member of Verlagsgruppe Random House GmbH

Prestel Verlag, Munich
Neumarkter Str. 28
D-81673 Munich

Prestel Publishing Ltd.
4 Bloomsbury Place
London WC1A 2QA

Prestel Publishing
900 Broadway, Suite 603
New York, NY 10003

www.prestel.de

www.prestel.com

www.prestel.com

Prestel books are available worldwide. Please contact your nearest bookseller or one of the above addresses for information concerning your local distributor.

Edited by: Martha Jay
Design and layout: Michael Schmölzl, agenten.und.freunde, Munich
Production: Nele Krüger
Art direction: Cilly Klotz
Origination: Reproline Mediateam, Munich
Printing and binding: Printer Trento, Trento

Verlagsgruppe Random House FSC-DEU-0100
The FSC-certified paper Eurobulk has been supplied by Papier Union, Germany.

ISBN 978-3-7913-7062-0